When Silence Speaks

Copyright

2022 Asif Shakoor, All Rights Reserved
ISBN 978-1-387-45062-6

Dedication

I dedicate this book to my patients whose darkest moments have become the voice of my soul. May the healing spirit of empathy and compassion remain the sole purpose of my healing role.

Preface

The deepest meaning in life is to live in a world of simplicity. The great wealth of this world will leave us poor if we are swept away by the luxury, the pleasures, and the power of what it can give us. The most satisfying life is lived for a purpose. To achieve richness in life it must be meaningful, and to accomplish it not for fame, not for fortune but for the growth of our human spirit. We are born to self-reflect on finding meaning in who we are, what we are, and why we are here in this world. The sole purpose of writing this third book was to give us a conscious voice to strive for Self-dignity and humility. In the spirit of a Sufi Mystic, poetry becomes the vision of truth that moves us toward the light to overcome the darkness of reality. In our deep silent moments, the voice of our soul will reveal the true wisdom of our existence. This third book, When Silence Speaks reflects the uncertainty of our lives in a world that has lost its moral voice and vision. Words have the power to liberate our spirit from the web of life and give us the courage to overcome the challenges we will face in our lives. Life is a journey and if we walk and continue to walk whether in pain, suffering, success, or failure then we have achieved our life's wisdom and given our silent words a voice for the world to hear.

The power of words moves our spirit to seek the deepest meaning of existence, but it is the act of what we do and how we live that gives life its colorful substance.

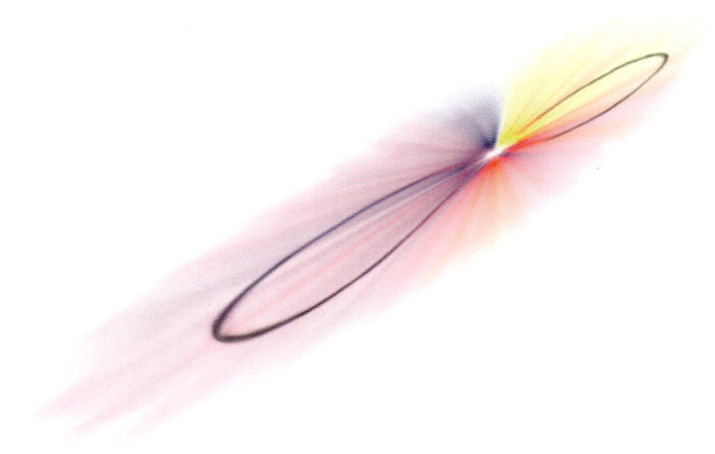

The hand's touch burns in the glow of consciousness. The darkness of this world blankets your form as your spirit grows in the candle's eye.

It is love for life which moves us toward the light, the wisdom in hope that never dies.

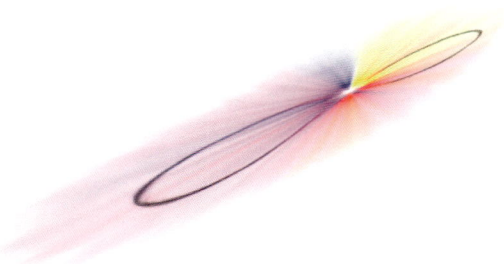

The night falls quietly into your dreams but in the light of dawn, you are awakened by the soft whisper of the summer breeze.
"Will you come into the light," the echo calls to the wind, "and follow me, please."

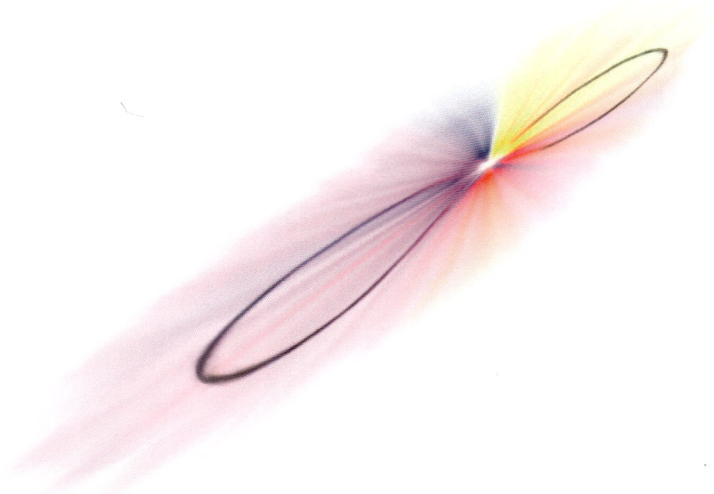

You come to me to cut me down, but I wait for you with open arms. You leave me with my burden so deep that I shed my leaves totally broken-hearted. I have become the tree that will grow deep in your forest. In my lonely moments, I have walked these mountains with heavy steps. I have become the seed that will grow into your human soul.

You are the bud in this garden of roses. The wind is the soul of a mother, and the light a father's true love. Will you sleep in tranquility and breathe in your fragrance slowly and deeply?
Your world is born in this mix of living colors; the beauty of the world delights in your senses.
The universe is never whole until your mind is one with it.

You are the child of this Earth, as you circle in hope, longing for your one true love. The full moon gives face to the mystical sky, a white pearl to the naked eye. Will you look through the darkness of this world to seek the moon that touches the sky?
Will you come out of your old ways and let Nature become your spiritual teacher?

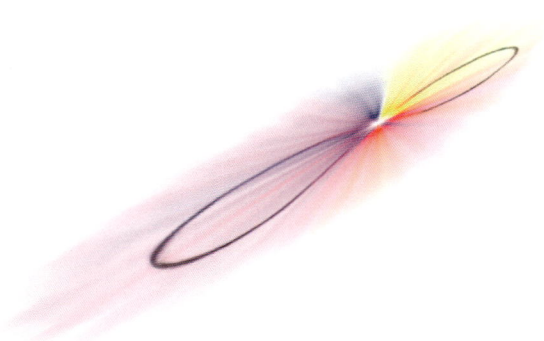

We are but a drop in the ocean
flowing into the heart of one
who is our giver.

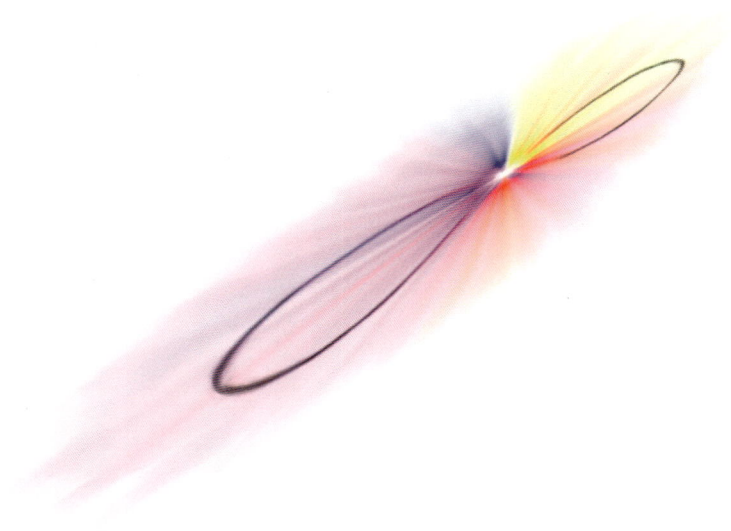

Will we let light awaken our mind and burn into our world the fragrance of existence?
The light has come strong and fast to bring us closer to the secrets of the universe.
Oh, light!
What is the impulse that moves you far and wide?
How do you spread your colors on the canvas of this world?

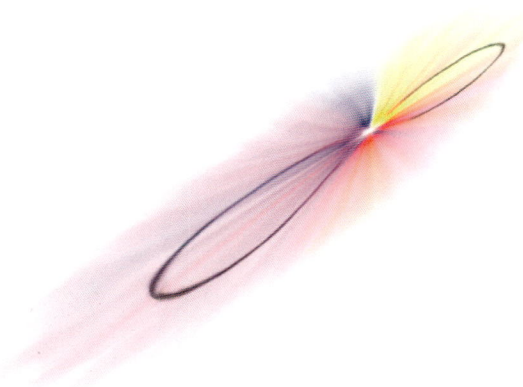

Memories fly in the sky like butterflies in the open breeze; silent dreams breaking through the night only the inner-eye can see.
Half-forgotten moments etched into playful days pressed on the sands of time, as childhood wisdom grows into the human voice like a playful melody in rhythm and rhyme.
In love we were born; so much love is in our hearts.
How much life have we spent in moments of reflection to give our spirit a head start?

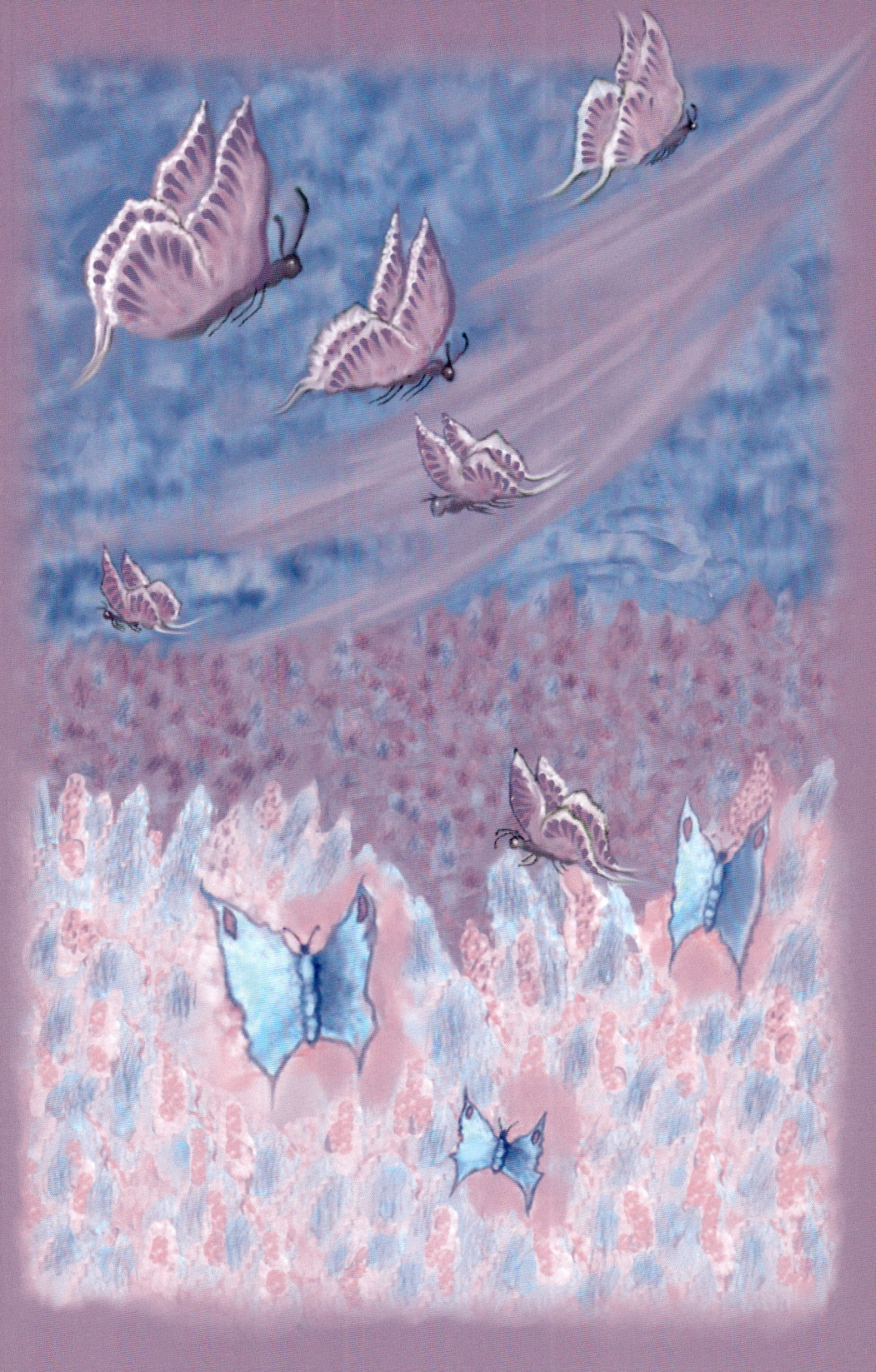

We hold in our hands
the strings of life;
it swings the pendulum
from past to present.
Rest in this "now" moment
to enjoy the breeze that
makes the journey
warm and pleasant.

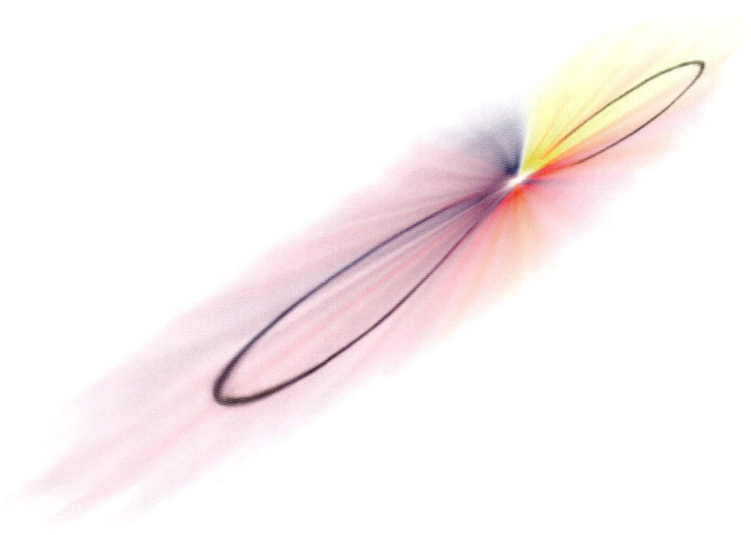

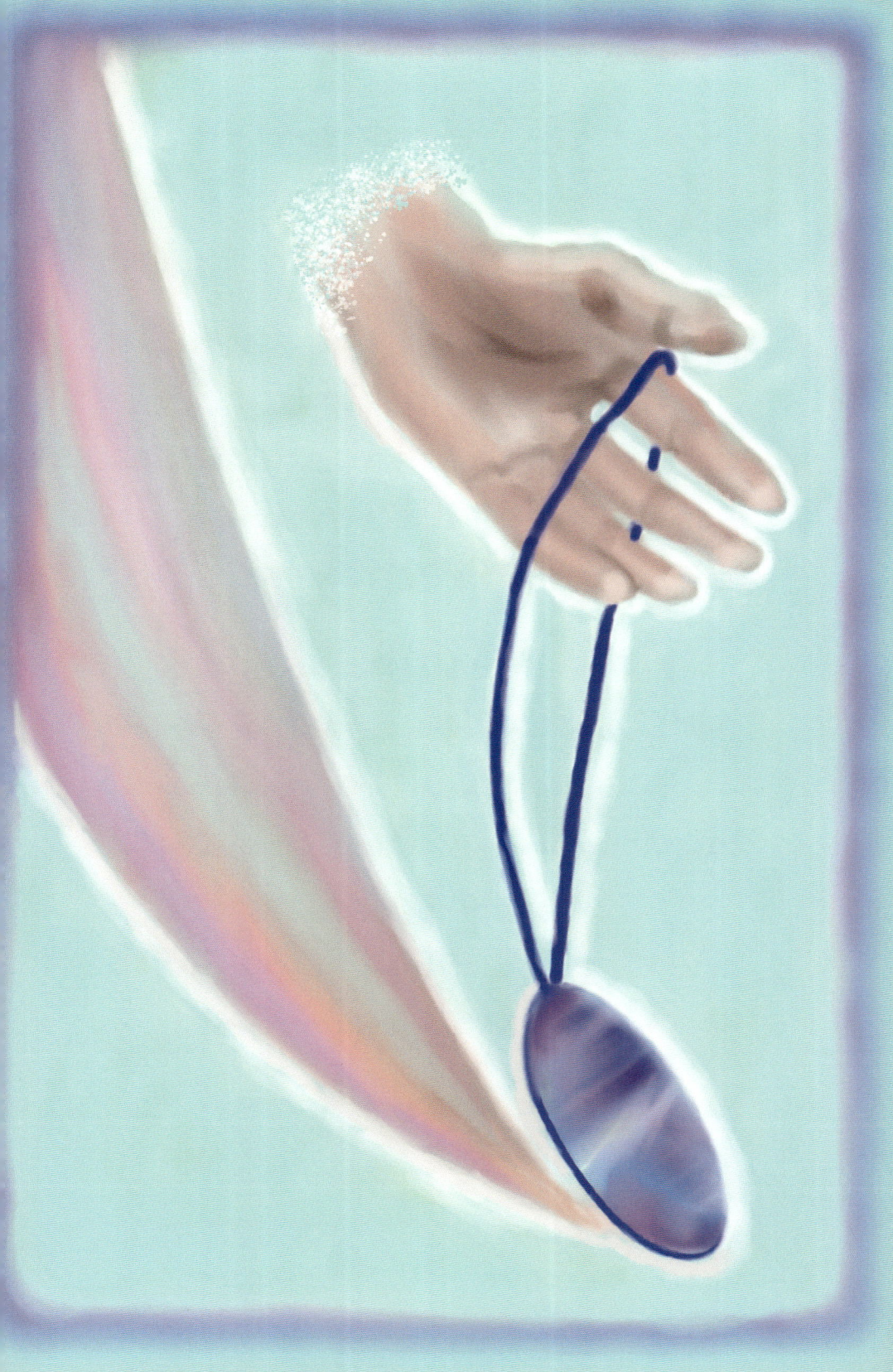

The wise walk the straight path to ease their burden, but a fool will walk with heavy steps and wander in all directions.

How beautiful is life's wisdom which helps us to see our foolish ways? How will we walk through darkness
when our vision has gone astray?

A pebble of reality
is released from the hand
and moves the surface under
the stillness of a pond.
Waves of conscious
emotions move the soul
onto the shore
and beyond.

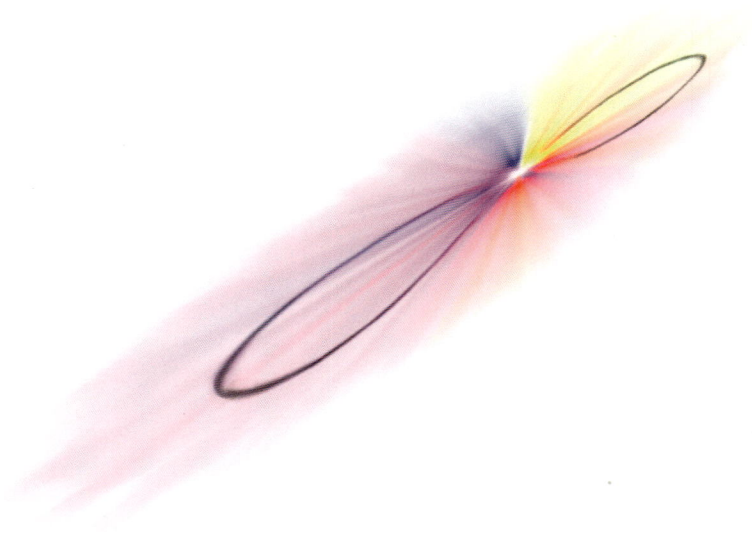

Can we breathe in the vastness of space and hold our breath in wonder?
Can we give truth the doors to our imagination?

A thousand stars sparkle in glory to burn away the darkness of the mystical night.
How far must we journey to trace the path to love?

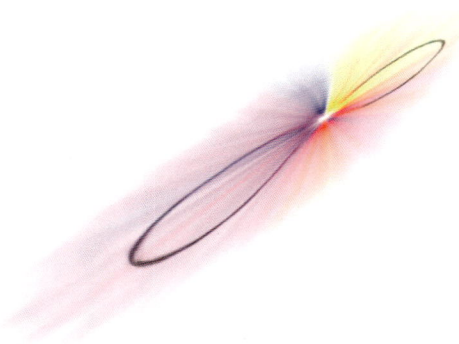

The human spirit burns with
the passion
of being human, but the
noble soul will never let that
be.
Will we open our eyes to the
will of being
and give wings to the spirit
that wills it to be free?

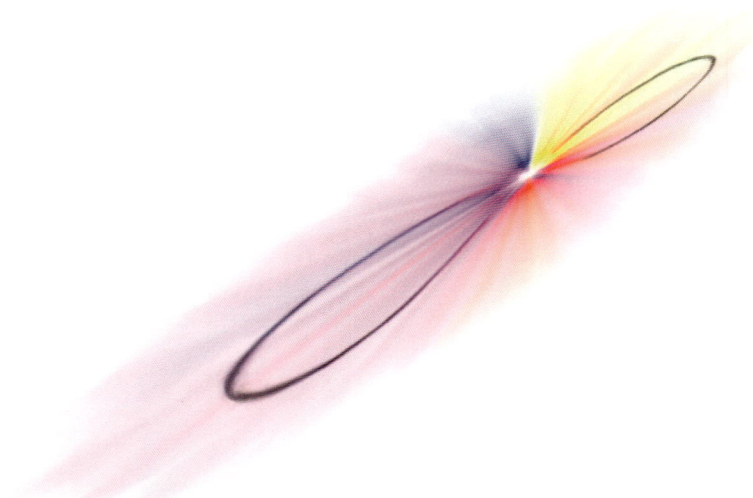

Reflection

There will be no foresight in our Life's journey when we continue on our destructive path with a glaring pace in our steps.

There will be no insight into our actions when we continue to make the same mistakes in chasing dreams that don't exist in reality.

There will be no foresight when we don't think before we act and act without thinking of the consequences of our actions.

No insight will be gained when we move forward and backward with hesitancy in our mind's sense of direction.

humanity when we give up our values for the values of others by sacrificing our individuality.

There will be no insight into our wisdom when we don't believe in what we say and don't live in our truthful ways.

Our faith will have no foresight when we can't distinguish between good and evil that our conscious eye sees so clearly.

A moment's insight is sometimes worth a life's experience.
Oliver Wendell Holmes Sr.